How Life Science Works

HOW DO MONARCH BUTTERFLIES FIND THEIR WAY HOME?

KIP ALMASY

PowerKiDS press.
New York

Published in 2018 by The Rosen Publishing Group, Inc.
29 East 21st Street, New York, NY 10010

First Edition

Editor: Theresa Morlock
Book Design: Tanya Dellaccio

Photo Credits: Cover, back cover, pp. 1, 3–4, 6–10, 12–14, 16–24 Mike Vande Ven Jr/Shutterstock.com; p. 5 Noradoa/Shutterstock.com; p. 7 (top) CANARYLUC/Shutterstock.com; p. 7 (bottom) Ed Reschke/Photolibrary/Getty Images; p. 8 Cathy Keifer/Shutterstock.com; p. 9 (top) Elliotte Rusty Harold/Shutterstock.com; p. 9 (bottom) William Booth/Shutterstock.com; p. 10 RHONDA ROBERTS/Shutterstock.com; p. 11 Sheryl Williams/Shutterstock.com; p. 13 (top) StevenRussellSmithPhotos/Shutterstock.com; p. 13 (bottom) mhgstan/Shutterstock.com; p. 15 JHVEPhoto/Shutterstock.com; p. 16 davidhoffmann photography/Shutterstock.com; p. 17 (top) Stephen Dalton/Minden Pictures/Getty Images; p. 17 (bottom) Angel DiBilio/Shutterstock.com; p. 19 (top) https://commons.wikimedia.org/wiki/File:Monarch_Butterfly_Danaus_plexippus_Tagged_Closeup_3008px.jpg; p. 19 (bottom) Richard Ellis/Getty Images News/Getty Images; p. 20 Chuchawan/Shutterstock.com; p. 21 (top) dejavubymarciachase/Shutterstock.com; p. 21 (bottom) Deborah Harrison/Photographer's Choice/Getty Images.

Cataloging-in-Publication Data
Names: Almasy, Kip.
Title: How do monarch butterflies find their way home? / Kip Almasy.
Description: New York : PowerKids Press, 2018. | Series: How life science works | Includes index.
Identifiers: ISBN 9781508156482 (pbk.) | ISBN 9781508156420 (library bound) | ISBN 9781508156307 (6 pack)
Subjects: LCSH: Monarch butterfly–Juvenile literature.
Classification: LCC QL561.D3 A44 2018 | DDC 595.78'9–dc23

Manufactured in the United States of America

CPSIA Compliance Information: Batch #BS17PK For Further Information contact Rosen Publishing, New York, New York at 1-800-237-9932

CONTENTS

BEAUTIFUL BUTTERFLIES

Monarch butterflies have always captured people's hearts and imaginations. With their stunning orange wings, pretty patterns, and spotted bodies, these insects are delightful to look at. But the beauty of monarchs is only part of what makes them so amazing. Throughout their lives, monarch butterflies go through a special journey.

Monarchs are the only butterflies that make a two-way **migration**. Their flapping wings can carry them across distances of up to 3,000 miles (4,828 km)! Monarchs living in the eastern part of North America fly south to Mexico for the winter. How do they find their way there and back?

The word "monarch" means the king or queen of a country. It's believed that monarch butterflies might have been named after Prince William of Orange, later the King of England, because of their color.

LIFE CYCLE OF A BUTTERFLY

The monarch butterfly's life cycle is made up of four stages: egg, larva, pupa, and adult. Monarchs lay their eggs during spring and summer. Females lay a single egg on each milkweed plant. The eggs are attached to milkweed leaves by a special glue the mother makes in her body.

Monarch eggs are only about the size of a pencil tip! Female butterflies can lay 700 eggs in two to five weeks. After about four days, the eggs hatch. Once hatched, the butterflies enter the larva, or caterpillar, stage. Monarch caterpillars have black, white, and yellow stripes. All of the butterfly's growth happens during the larva stage.

MONARCH EGG

Monarch mothers don't stick around to take care of their babies when they hatch. The little caterpillars are all on their own!

Monarch caterpillars spend the first two weeks of their lives eating as much milkweed as they can. They use tiny hooks on their legs to hold onto the leaves or stems of milkweed plants. They have six pairs of eyes but very poor vision. They depend on their **antennae** to help them find food.

As they eat, caterpillars grow and become too big for their skin. They **molt** their old skin when it becomes too tight. The new skin layer beneath hardens to protect their body. Caterpillars eat the skin they molt. The time between molting is called an instar. Caterpillars go through five instars.

A MONARCH'S CATERPILLAR STAGE LASTS FOR ABOUT TWO WEEKS.

METAMORPHOSIS

When it's ready to enter the pupa stage, the caterpillar spins a silk mat. It hangs upside down from the mat, attached by a stem from its body called a cremaster. It then molts for the last time, revealing a green layer of skin that hardens to protect its body while it develops into a butterfly.

A butterfly pupa is called a chrysalis. Inside the chrysalis, the butterfly changes to its adult form. After about two weeks, an adult butterfly emerges. A monarch's change from a caterpillar to a butterfly is known as metamorphosis. Metamorphosis occurs when a living thing goes through a complete change in form or body.

THE SILK COVERING AROUND A MOTH IN ITS PUPA STAGE IS CALLED A COCOON. BUTTERFLIES DO NOT MAKE COCOONS.

ADULT MONARCH BUTTERFLIES

When monarch butterflies first emerge from their chrysalis, their wings are wrinkled and wet. It takes about an hour for their wings to dry and unfold to their full size. An adult monarch's wingspan is about 3.5 to 4 inches (9.4 to 10.5 cm).

Most adult monarch butterflies only live for a few weeks. They spend their lives feeding on **nectar** and finding mates, or partners for making babies. The only monarch butterflies that live longer than five weeks are those that are born at the end of summer. These monarchs will make the long journey to Mexico.

FEMALE MONARCH

You can tell male monarchs apart from females by the black spot on each lower wing.

MALE MONARCH

MIGRATION TRIGGERS

Monarch butterflies live throughout the United States and in lower parts of Canada. Most live east of the Rocky Mountains. Those living east of the Rocky Mountains head south to Mexico for the winter and those to the west of the Rocky Mountains fly south to California.

How do butterflies know when it's time to fly south? Their **instinct** to migrate is **triggered** by temperatures dropping, days becoming shorter, and milkweed plants aging. These conditions cause the life cycle of migratory monarchs to pause. That way they don't mate and lay eggs until they've reached warmer southern **habitats**.

A PAUSE IN AN INSECT'S DEVELOPMENT IS CALLED DIAPAUSE. THIS CAN ALSO HAPPEN WITH OTHER ANIMALS.

TAKING WING

Migrating monarchs cover between 25 and 30 miles (40.2 and 48.3 km) each day. The distance is affected by the weather and the amount of wind, which they use to help them fly. Sometimes they're able to **glide**, only flapping their wings every 20 to 30 feet (6 to 9.1 m).

Active flight uses more energy than gliding. Butterflies can sometimes fly at speeds of 12 miles (19.3 km) per hour or more. During their journey, butterflies face dangers such as bad weather and predators. If they're able to survive storms and predators, the journey to Mexico takes monarchs about 2.5 months to complete.

Monarch butterflies stay warm by **clustering** together.

OVERWINTERING

In Mexico, monarchs **roost** in fir trees in the mountains. They then complete their usual life cycle, find mates, and lay eggs.

None of the butterflies that make the migration south live long enough to fly back home. They begin their migration north in early spring, laying eggs in northern Mexico and the southern United States. The eggs become a new generation of monarchs that continues the journey north. The complete monarch migration takes about four generations. Monarchs that return to the north are the great-grandchildren of those that migrated south to Mexico. Although they've never made the trip before, these butterflies somehow manage to find their way home.

Scientists put tags on monarch butterflies so that we can learn more about their migration patterns by tracking them.

THE MYSTERY OF NAVIGATION

Monarchs use two tools to help them **navigate** on their journey–the position of the sun and their circadian clock. A circadian clock is the body's way of telling a living thing what time of day it is based on clues from the world around it.

The sun rises in the east and sets in the west. A butterfly's circadian clock tells it whether it's morning (when the sun is rising) or evening (when the sun is setting). The time plus the sun's position shows it which direction it's flying toward. A butterfly heading south would fly with the rising sun to the east on its left.

SOME SCIENTISTS BELIEVE THAT THEY CAN SENSE EARTH'S **MAGNETIC FIELD,** WHICH GUIDES THEM WHEN THEY CAN'T SEE THE SUN.

INCREDIBLE INSECTS

From their metamorphosis to their migration, monarch butterflies are an awesome example of life science in action. Though small and **delicate**, they are able to survive the many challenges of migration. Unfortunately, they have been put at risk by habitat loss and **global warming**. The changing temperatures caused by global warming upset the butterflies' migration patterns. Pesticides, or chemicals made to kill weeds and bugs, harm milkweed plants, which monarchs need to survive.

By taking action to protect butterfly habitats, planting milkweeds, and educating others about monarch butterflies, we can help make sure that these beautiful creatures continue to survive for years to come.

GLOSSARY

antennae: Thin, rod-like feelers located on the head of certain animals.

cluster: To gather together in a group.

delicate: Easily broken or damaged.

glide: To move or fly smoothly with little effort.

global warming: The increase in the world's temperature that's believed to be caused by human actions.

habitat: The natural home for plants, animals, and other living things.

instinct: The feeling a creature has that helps it know what to do.

magnetic field: The area around a magnet where its pull is felt.

migration: The movement of animals from one place to another as the seasons change.

molt: To shed skin.

navigate: To find one's way.

nectar: A sweet liquid found in flowers.

roost: To settle for rest or sleep.

trigger: To cause something to happen.

INDEX

WEBSITES

Due to the changing nature of Internet links, PowerKids Press has developed an online list of websites related to the subject of this book. This site is updated regularly. Please use this link to access the list:
www.powerkidslinks.com/ls/mon